£1.50

Christian, the Hugging Lion

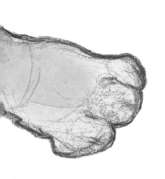

D1335977

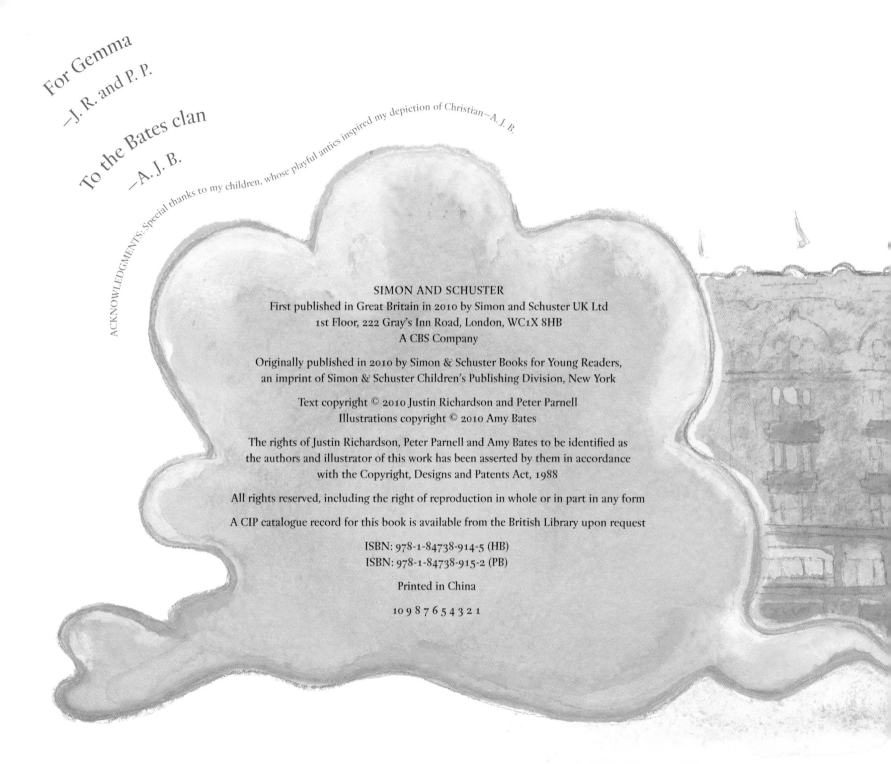

For Gemma
—J. R. and P. P.

To the Bates clan
—A. J. B.

ACKNOWLEDGMENTS: Special thanks to my children, whose playful antics inspired my depiction of Christian—A. J. B.

SIMON AND SCHUSTER
First published in Great Britain in 2010 by Simon and Schuster UK Ltd
1st Floor, 222 Gray's Inn Road, London, WC1X 8HB
A CBS Company

Originally published in 2010 by Simon & Schuster Books for Young Readers,
an imprint of Simon & Schuster Children's Publishing Division, New York

Text copyright © 2010 Justin Richardson and Peter Parnell
Illustrations copyright © 2010 Amy Bates

The rights of Justin Richardson, Peter Parnell and Amy Bates to be identified as
the authors and illustrator of this work has been asserted by them in accordance
with the Copyright, Designs and Patents Act, 1988

A CIP catalogue record for this book is available from the British Library upon request

ISBN: 978-1-84738-914-5 (HB)
ISBN: 978-1-84738-915-2 (PB)

Printed in China

10 9 8 7 6 5 4 3 2 1

Christian, the Hugging Lion

BY Justin Richardson AND Peter Parnell

ILLUSTRATED BY Amy June Bates

Harrods

Simon & Schuster Books for Young Readers

Many years ago, the most famous store in London made the world a promise. At Harrods you could buy absolutely anything you wanted. Anything!

What would you like? Chocolate tea? Silk pyjamas? A coconut from Brazil? How about a racing car or a yacht with five white sails?

"Yessir," the clerk would say. "I'll get that right away!"

Better still, at Harrods you could buy the most unusual pets.

"I'd like a camel, if you don't mind."

"Certainly, madam. One hump or two?"

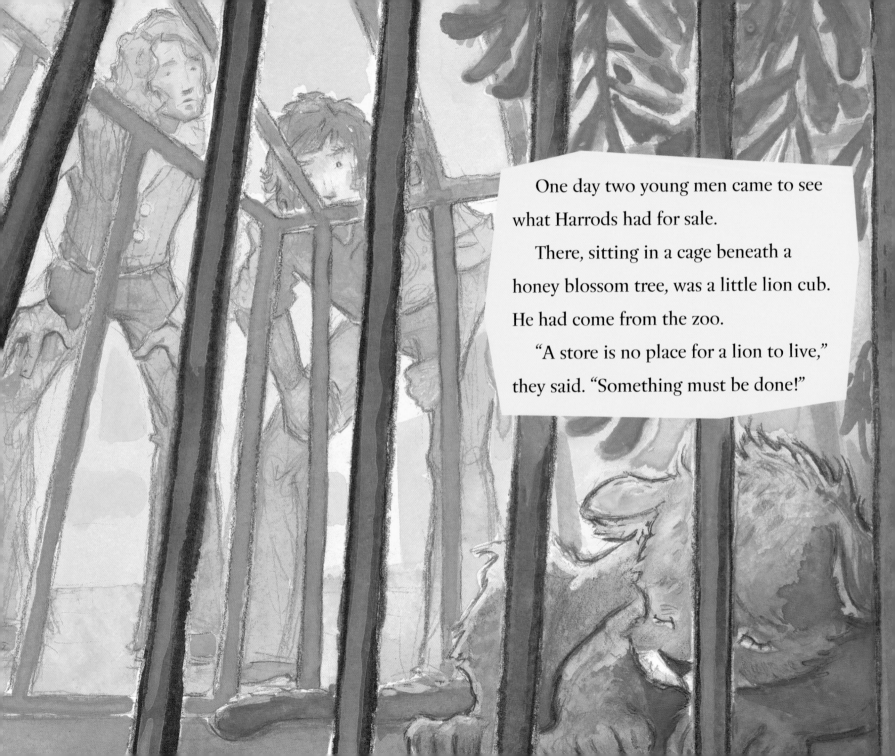

One day two young men came to see
what Harrods had for sale.

There, sitting in a cage beneath a
honey blossom tree, was a little lion cub.
He had come from the zoo.

"A store is no place for a lion to live,"
they said. "Something must be done!"

And so Ace and John bought him and took him back
to their apartment. "We'll call him Christian," they said.

Christian curled up between his new friends on their
paisley sofa. He seemed very happy to have found a home.

Christian liked to roll and play and chase his toys under the furniture. He spent hours peering through the window at the birds outside.

And he loved to put his paws on Ace's and John's shoulders and do something that wild lions never do. He hugged them.

Christian became a very well-behaved little cub.

Most of the time.

After all, he was still a lion.

Ace and John took Christian with them everywhere they went.

When they went for a stroll in the morning, they paraded him down the Kings Road.

They played with him in the churchyard.

They ate lunch with him in their favourite restaurant,
where the chef served Christian in high style.

And they even took Christian to the pub.
Christian was very friendly to everyone
he met, although sometimes his hugs were
a little clumsy.

Christian loved to take in the sights of London from the back seat of Ace and John's car. He loved to picnic at the beach on the English Channel and feel the sun on his back, although the water was disagreeably cold.

Come on in, Christian!

Most of all, Christian loved being with Ace and John. The three of them had become the most unusual family in all of London.

After a year of Christian's eating and playing and growing, it wasn't quite as comfortable for Ace and John to snuggle with him on their paisley sofa.

Should they get a bigger sofa? Or move to a bigger apartment?

Would they have to take Christian to the zoo?

"No!" Ace and John decided.

"Lions belong in the wild."

Christian was happy in London, but Ace and John knew he'd be happier in Africa. So they made a plan to fly there.

Christian would have to travel inside a wooden crate.
He didn't seem to like the idea. Ace and John climbed in to
show him how comfortable it could be. "It's lovely in here!"

Reluctantly, Christian agreed. And every day
he practised spending a little more time in the
crate. It was going to be a very long trip.

Finally the day came to fly.

When the three of them arrived in Kenya, a crowd gathered.
Everyone was surprised to see a lion who could ride in a plane.
"A lion from London?"

Ace and John drove Christian to meet Mr Adamson,
who taught lions how to live in the wild. They were
worried. "How will Christian manage without
the churchyard to play in or the chef
to fix his lunch?"

"Leave him to me," Mr Adamson said with a smile.

And so they did.

Christian looked around. The sky was wider than he had ever
seen, even over Hyde Park. There were many more birds than
outside his favourite window. And in the distance he saw gazelles
grazing. They made his nose twitch and his hind legs feel springy.

Should he run after them? Was that allowed in Africa?
A breeze tickled Christian's fur. The air was dry and smelled
of honey blossoms. It filled his chest and stirred a feeling that
rattled up to his mouth and came out as a strange new sound.

Back in London, Ace and John missed Christian's hugs. They drove in their car and went on picnics and ate at their favourite restaurant. But it wasn't the same without him.

Finally, they called Mr Adamson.

"How is Christian?" they asked.

"Very well, indeed! He's gone off into the wild."

Could they visit him?

"We could try to find him. But he may not remember you. Christian is a grown-up lion now, with cubs of his own."

"Let's go!" they said.

When they arrived in Kenya, what did they see?

Christian!

Their old friend took a long look at them.

And then . . .

They were together again! Christian and Ace and John played all day until the evening sun began to slip behind the trees. Then they settled down for a quiet night's sleep under the Kenyan stars.

Ace and John knew that in the morning Christian would go back to his new lion family. But for that night the three of them curled up together just like they used to. Cosy and snug and, of course, hugging.

Authors' Note

ALL OF THE EVENTS IN THIS STORY ARE TRUE. Christian was born to a long line of zoo lions in 1969 at the Ilfracombe Zoo in Devon, England. He was three months old when John Rendall and Ace Bourke purchased him from Harrods' exotic pet department for 250 guineas — about £3000 in today's money.

Christian did, in fact, visit a restaurant and a pub and play ball in a churchyard. But he spent most of his days a floor or two below Ace and John's apartment in the furniture shop where they both worked. The real Christian is world-famous for his hugs. Still, hugging is not something you ought to try with just any lion.

After the reunion depicted in this book, Ace and John visited Christian one more time. By then, he had grown from a 16kg pet cub to the 225kg leader of a pride on the banks of the Tana River. He had become the very first member of his family in many generations to live free in Africa. During that visit Ace, John, and Christian played happily together before saying a final good-bye. The three never met again, but thanks to a now-famous video of their reunion that appeared on the Internet in 2008, their friendship lives on.